Home Econ
University of akron

FURNITURE
YESTERDAY AND TODAY

Corner in Room from Petersburg, Va.,
American Wing, Metropolitan Museum of
Art, showing wing chair and stool with
Sheraton reeded leg; Sheraton arm and side
chairs; an unusual fire screen

FURNITURE
YESTERDAY AND TODAY

*The Principal Periods of Furniture
with Numerous Illustrations
of the Best Historical and
Modern Examples, by*

JULIUS F. GAYLER, R.A.

MEMBER AMERICAN INSTITUTE OF ARCHITECTS

With a Special Note on
FINISHES

1926
CURRIER & HARFORD · LIMITED
NEW YORK

CONTENTS

LIST OF ILLUSTRATIONS

All the photographic illustrations in
this book are shown by courtesy of
the Metropolitan Museum of Art,
New York City

I

A Brief History of Furniture With Its Principal Periods

THE story of furniture is linked with the story of man's development and his rise from the savage state through the various stages of civilization. The caveman probably used large stones or boulders for chairs and tables until a more progressive spirit happened to find the use of trunks of trees more comfortable and better adapted to the purpose. From tree trunks, possibly some genius, with a recollection of finding restful seats in trees while a boy, evolved the idea of a crotch formed by the trunks and limbs and so obtained a rest for the back and the result was the first crude chair. And our early ancestor who, with a stone hatchet, first fashioned and formed the seats and backs to fit the human form, is as worthy of a monument as is the one who first cut a dugout from a log and made the first canoe. The earliest known examples of the chair were developments of the thrones of the kings and the nobility, who were the only ones to whom this luxury was allowed. Tables undoubtedly developed from logs laid on other logs, or later, on rough trestles. Needless to say, all examples of these early, crude pieces are lost in the mists of time, as are the ones showing the development from them to our earliest known examples of furniture.

An interesting fact is that the oldest pieces of furniture preserved to us represent a very high state of development in the art and had a great deal of influence on at least one of the later styles. The earliest examples of wooden furniture now extant are the wonderful pieces made by the Egyptians, preserved through these thousands of years because of the dry climate and because they were placed in the sacred tombs of the kings and nobility for use in their future life. The dry climate protected them from the dampness so fatal to wooden

Fig. 1. Egyptian Chair, X Type (King Tutankhamen)   Fig. 2. Queen Tiy Chair. (Type from which Empire Style was derived)   Fig. 3. Roman Chair

furniture and its finish, and their secret resting places from the despoilers and vandals. Some of these, such as the pieces found in Tutankhamen's tomb, are in as perfect condition as if fresh from the maker's hands, and show that the Egyptians had developed the art of furniture making to the same high plane as they had architecture, sculpture and mural decoration. The resemblance between some of the chairs, such as those of the parents of Queen Tiy, about 3300 years old, to the Empire style, is striking, and suggests the origin of this comparatively modern style, which is the result of Napoleon's campaign in Egypt.

In Tutankhamen's tomb were found chairs very similar to the Savonarola chairs of the Italian Renaissance. There is no possibility of a suggestion that the Renaissance artists drew their inspirations from the Egyptians, as at that time the Egyptian examples were still buried

Fig. 4. Savonarola Chair

in the thousands of years' accumulation of the sands of the desert. The reasonable assumption is that the Greeks copied this type of chair from the Egyptians, the Romans from the Greeks, and the Fourteenth to the Seventeenth Century Italians from the Romans. There are in existence chairs made by the Romans which show the connecting link. It is true that these are of bronze, but their very existence proves that wooden ones of the same type must also have been in use. Wooden chairs, by their very nature, could not have withstood so well the ravages of time and for this reason only the bronze ones have been preserved to us.

These early examples are interesting to us historically and on account of the thrill we feel at finding such perfectly preserved records of the life of a people so long past. Egyptian furniture, however, except for odd pieces, is not suitable for modern interior decoration and we are more concerned with the comparatively recent examples developed under conditions more

[11]

Fig. 5   Fig. 6

Fig. 5. Italian Renaissance Arm Chair. Note the stretchers at the floor. In the early heavy furniture these were needed for strength; later they were made lighter and ornamental or were dispensed with altogether.

Fig. 6. Walnut Chair, English, about 1685

Fig. 7   Fig. 8

Fig. 7. Walnut Arm Chair, English, 1702-1714.

Fig. 8. Windsor Chair, in pine and maple with hickory spokes. This type of chair was the model for the popular Windsor chair of today.

nearly resembling our own. These may be roughly classified as follows:

Italian Renaissance
Spanish Renaissance
French Renaissance
The later French: Louis XIV, XV, XVI and
    Empire
Dutch
The English Styles: Tudor, Elizabethan, Jacobean, William and Mary, Queen Anne
The products of the Master Craftsmen: Chippendale, The Adam Brothers, Hepplewhite and Sheraton
Our own Colonial

The above subdivisions of the early English styles are so called to correspond with the era, the reigning houses or the furniture designers of the times. Many writers divide them into the Oak Period, Walnut Period and Mahogany Period, from the woods used, the designs of the furniture being always modified to meet the character of material in which the designers worked.

The more modern Mission and Golden Oak Periods are interesting only as illustrating that furniture, which relies almost wholly on the appeal that it is "different" or "odd," and has no real merit of design or finish, cannot last. Abraham Lincoln's remark to the effect that "if people like that kind of a thing, that is the thing that they will like," applies to these so-called styles. It is interesting to artists and designers that the modern trend is directed farther from them and turning more towards all period furniture honestly made.

[13]

This means that "Better Homes" can have furniture worthy of them, and by "Better Homes" is meant not merely expensive homes. It costs no more to build the humble cottage in good taste than it does to build it in poor taste, and simple furniture can be as attractive in its way as more elaborate pieces, and costs no more —probably less—than the mission or golden oak monstrosities. Recent adaptations of oak in modern furniture reproducing the darker shades of early English, Jacobean and William and Mary periods are excellent.

Italian Renaissance furniture: This style, Fourteenth to Seventeenth Century, was, as the name implies, one of the results of the awakening from the Dark Ages. As in painting, sculpture and architecture, the artists were throwing off restraint and in their work were expressing the joy of living. The furniture of this period is dignified and formal, as suitable to the palaces of the times, although simple pieces were also beautifully done.

The tables were generally octagonal or long, of the pedestal type or supported on legs, with stretchers and carved or turned supports. The moldings were architectural and the elaborate carving or massive simplicity, together with a wonderful sense of proportion, makes this style of furniture very suitable for formal rooms and halls.

Fig 9. Italian Renaissance Table—Octagonal with Pedestal

Their chairs are of the Savonarola type, so called from the beautiful examples in Savonarola's cell at San Marco, Florence; and the formal high or low back chairs, with or without arms, upholstered in wonderful Italian stuffs of the period. In some of the larger pieces there was an architectural bracket, flat on the floor, placed on the front leg, and stretchers from front to rear legs were also characteristic of this period.

Most interesting in the work of this period were the chests, the forerunner of the "marriage chest," "hope chest" and cedar chest of the later periods. These were sometimes low so that they could be used as seats, and often high and used as side tables. They were generally long and narrow and more often elaborately carved. The panels themselves in some of the larger pieces were enriched with medallions of paintings similar to the religious and other paintings of the period. The early examples had distinctly a Gothic feeling. This style the Italians were slow to follow, Italian Gothic differing in spirit from that of the countries farther north, and being characterized by greater formality.

Wall cabinets, higher than the chests, with panelled

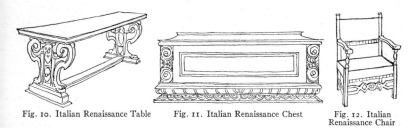

Fig. 10. Italian Renaissance Table   Fig. 11. Italian Renaissance Chest   Fig. 12. Italian Renaissance Chair

doors, console columns or elaborately carved supports, and answering the purpose of the later sideboards, curio cabinets or writing desks, were interesting objects of this time. The beds were the four-post type or low beds panelled and ornamented. Often they were on a raised platform.

[15]

The wood used in this period was almost exclusively the native walnut of even grain with very little figure, a wood admirably suited to carving and elaboration, with a dull, waxed finish that mellowed with age.

The Spanish Renaissance furniture was, as was the  Spanish Renaissance architecture and painting, similar to the Italian of this time but even richer in detail, often to excess. It was characterized by elaboration and the use of beautiful stuffs and ornamented leather.

Fig. 13. Louis XVI
Chair

The French Renaissance furniture is well worthy of study. It is an adaptation of the Italian Renaissance, as intercourse between these two countries was very considerable at that time, with the result that as in architecture the Italian feeling is very evident. This was all the stronger as Italian workmen, notably Benvenuto Cellini and Leonardo da Vinci, and other artists, were brought to their country by the French.

The later French Periods, Louis XIV and XV, are an expression of the lives and extravagant tastes of the kings and nobility of that time and are characterized by excessive rococo carving and ornaments. The woodwork of the furniture was generally gilded. This style was much in vogue in this country twenty or thirty years ago, and extensively used in elaborate residences, ballrooms, hotels and for similar purposes. But the style is not adaptable to the modern home. The

Fig. 14. Rococo Pier Table

Louis XVI style was more restrained and worthy of study and admiration. It was influenced by the Classic Revival from Italy and the style is therefore much more subdued than that of Louis XIV or Louis XV, and the ornament and lines were of a more sober and dignified character. The woodwork was sometimes gilded but more often painted, often in several tones of the same color. The English styles of the time, and following the above periods of French, were influenced to a great extent by them but were modified and subdued to more restful and livable lines.

Fig. 15. French Empire Chair

The Empire style was characterized by elaborate brass or bronze ornaments, often gilded, applied to the woodwork; a principle not to be copied, as true design should strive to ornament the construction with the same material rather than to enrich it by applying an entirely foreign substance.

The Dutch Period of furniture is well worthy of study not only on account of the splendid examples still extant but more particularly as it was the forerunner from which the later English styles were to a great extent developed. The marquetry work done in this period has never been surpassed.

The Tudor style, Sixteenth Century English, in its earliest periods was a continuation of the early Gothic style of which some examples still remain. During the latter part of this period, the Renaissance, the influence of which was felt a century later in England than on the continent, guided and inspired the craftsmen. With the encouragement from the Court, beautiful examples were produced.

The tables were generally long and ponderous with heavy tops, which fully justified the massive supports

Fig. 16. Room from Portsmouth, Rhode Island, showing early American furniture made previous to the time when mahogany came into use. This shows the Jacobean influence and is as fine as any English or American furniture of that period.

Fig. 17   Fig. 18

Fig. 17. Oak Highboy with Flemish Panelling. English, 1675-1700. Note the cabriole leg afterwards developed by Chippendale and other Eighteenth Century furniture makers.

Fig. 18. Gate Leg Table, 1675-1700. Walnut.

under them and the stretchers at the floor. The legs were massive and turned, of the type known as bulbous, with carving of classic type, or simple, gouged-out design, similar carving being applied to the other portions of the table.

The chairs were of the "X" type, sometimes entirely covered with material and showing the Italian influence, or of the turned type, often with triangular seats. Frequently, especially in the early part of the period, there were no chairs, but stools without backs or long benches of the character to correspond with the tables.

Previous to this time, that is, in the time of the Normans, benches and chests served the purpose of beds, the bedding being kept inside. Blocks or legs were put under these to keep them from the damp rushes they used to cover the floor. Like the beds of the Italian Renaissance, the elaborate beds of the Tudor Period were massive and ornamental, of the high four-post type with post similar to the bulbous

Fig. 19. Triangular Chair

Fig. 20. Tudor Table

Fig. 21. Tudor Bed

legs of the table, and generally elaborately carved.

The wood used in this period was the native English oak, and the examples preserved to us are of that soft, brown color and patine, the result of age and care, though the same result is nowadays obtainable in a few days by means of du Pont Duco, a recently developed finish. The construction was heavy and the parts were put together with mortise and tenon, held together by stout pins, generally of oak. There are no examples of veneer used at this time, as this was a later development, although in some cases inlay was used, pieces of holly or poplar being let into a background of black bog oak in a simple floral or geometrical design. This was the forerunner of the later marquetry work.

The Jacobean style, Seventeenth Century English, was known also as the style of the early English Renaissance. This was the result of further development of Renaissance ideals mingled with the ideals of the Flemings, then the traders and travelers whose country, the Netherlands, was the art center of Northern Europe. It should be borne in mind that it is not possible to define distinctly the line between the early examples of this and the later examples of the preceding style, as the transition was more or less gradual and certain characteristics are common to both. But whereas the Tudor Period was characterized in many cases by overcrowding and elaboration of ornament, more restraint is evident in the Jacobean, especially in the latter part. Lathe-turned ornaments, balusters and spindles were frequently applied to the woodwork instead of carving, these being often stained black in imitation of ebony, thus making a pleasing contrast with the background.

The tables in the early part of this period were similar to the heavy type of the Tudor Period, with bulbous legs. Later the refectory type of tables came into use with four or six legs, sometimes with turned balusters underneath, reminiscent of the Italian style. The gate leg table of oak was a development of this time, and many fine old examples are still preserved. These were of various sizes, some very small and some large enough to seat ten people. They were made generally with turned legs, although there are some examples extant with spiral legs. These tables were generally round or oval, and fitted with drop tops, one or two of the legs revolving so that the table could be used as a pier table.

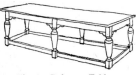
Fig. 22. Refectory Table

The chairs were of both the high and the low back type with or without arms. The legs of these chairs were frequently turned columns of modified classic feeling and later of the twisted type, as were the rungs. Velvet stuffs and cane were used for inserts in the backs and seats.

In the early part of this period the chests were of the heavy, massive type, with the fronts elaborately panelled or carved, becoming later, with legs turned or twisted, the forerunner of the high and low boy. The drawers were generally fitted with beautiful brass drop handles. To this period belongs also the couch with the adjustable head-rest, often with elaborately carved legs and stretchers. These were the forerunners of the later day-bed or chaise-longue.

Fig. 23. Day Bed

The Jacobean style marks the beginning of the use of walnut in English furniture, although there were many pieces, especially in the early portion of the period, in which oak was used. There were also pieces in which both were used, one wood for moldings and another for panelling. In some cases, an entire piece was oak except that the fronts of the drawers were veneered with beautifully grained walnut veneer. Changes from one wood to another are necessarily responsible for changes of style, due to the use of a new material, as the limitations and possibilities of the different woods determine the character of the design and ornament.

Fig. 24.
Jacobean Chair

The use of veneer was begun at this time. Previously it had not been possible to cut wood into planks less than an inch thick. With greater skill and advance in the cabinetmakers' art, it became possible to saw wood one-quarter of an inch thick, or even thinner. This opened a new field and made it possible to use beautifully grained wood full of knots, grain and burl, by gluing it to a background of some more stable wood, the richly grained wood, by its very nature, not being strong enough to use by itself as solid wood, owing to the imperfections which made it beautiful. These markings are the result of cutting the tree in rounds from the root of the tree to the branches, lengthwise at right angles to the wood—quartering, or cutting the tree at the crotch, which is the junction of the roots with the trunk, instead of sawing lengthwise into planks. There is an impression among some people that all modern furniture is veneered, whereas all antique furniture was made of solid wood and, therefore, is better. This is not the case. Antique and modern furniture are made both veneered and of solid material, depending on the design and period.

The William and Mary, and Queen Anne style of furniture, known also as the period of Dutch influence, was usually walnut, except for marquetry work. It was used both solid and veneered. Sometimes it was inlaid with different woods. It was a logical sequence and de-

Fig. 25.
William and Mary
Wing Chair

velopment of the previous style, modified by the ever-increasing influence from the Netherlands. This was particularly shown in the marquetry work, light woods, sometimes of several shades, being inlaid on a darker background in most intricate and pleasing designs. In some cases this arrangement was reversed, the darker woods being inlaid on lighter, thus producing even a richer effect. For this marquetry work various woods were used— holly, sycamore and rosewood being combined with darker woods. It is of interest to note that this marquetry work was contemporaneous with and influenced by the French buhl work, which consisted of tortoise-shell inlaid in or on brass.

The tall clock—"grandfather's clock"— made its first appearance at this time, as well as the chair with the cabriole leg, which was later so beautifully developed by Chippendale.

Fig. 26.
Corner Cabinet

Gate leg tables, lighter in detail than the previous ones, were made. These were both large and small, often with turned legs formed by turning the classic baluster upside down, thus forming a bell at the top. The tall clocks made at this time were often richly inlaid and their design with turned or twisted columns on either side of the clock face is so similar to the later mahogany clocks as to leave no doubt as to the source of inspiration for these later examples.

Chairs, with and without arms, included the simple cabriole leg chairs with seats covered with material; wing chairs entirely covered with material, except as to the legs; and those with inverted balusters or bell-shaped legs with carved stretchers and cane inserts in seats and backs. They were charming in their simplicity and graceful lines. But the most characteristic and elaborate pieces of this time were the cabinets. These were generally supported on twisted or carved legs; the upper doors and panels were enriched with marquetry and the cabinets were cunningly fitted with drawers having marquetry fronts and veneers of various woods.

Fig. 27.
Inverted Baluster

The desks and highboys were of the high and low type, and generally were enriched with veneers of especially selected woods, marquetry being then not so common.

Corner cabinets with mirrors or glazed doors for the display of china were of a character similar to the desks and cabinets. The beds were generally of the high post type, with thin classic columns at corners, although in some cases the rear columns were concealed by the curtains of rich materials, which were also used to cover the top. Dressing tables and mirrors, including small portable mirrors for the dressing tables, of various sizes and similar character, were also well represented in this style.

II

Eighteenth Century English Furniture Makers

WE now arrive at the most interesting period of English furniture—the period that produced the master craftsmen who were the makers of the best known and most beautiful furniture in all its history; beautiful, not only on account of the marvelous designs and skill of execution, but also on account of the use of a new wood—mahogany—a wood renowned for its beauty of grain and color, and its strong and lasting qualities. This wood comes from a slow-growing tree imported from the tropics.

Of all the designers of furniture of this time and kind the best known was Thomas Chippendale, whose name is always associated with the most wonderful furniture ever made. There seems to be some difference of opinion among the historians as to who was the first to use mahogany for furniture in England. One story is that the first log of this wood was sent to a Dr. Gibbon in London as a present from a friend in the West Indies about the year 1724. Finding it too hard and unworkable for use in the building of his house, Dr. Gibbon took a piece of it to Thomas Chippendale, a cabinetmaker with a shop near by, and out of it had him make a simple piece of furniture. Be that as it may, Chip-

Fig. 28   Fig. 29

Fig. 28. Mahogany Arm Chair, 1760-1770. This is in the style of Chippendale's later work. Note the straight instead of the cabriole leg.

Fig. 29. Ladder Back Chair, 1765-1775. Mahogany.

Fig. 30   Fig. 31

Fig. 30. Mahogany Side Chair, 1770. Chippendale Style.

Fig. 31. Mahogany Arm Chair, shield back, and with the characteristic grace and lightness of Hepplewhite.

pendale was the first to appreciate the beauty and possibilities of this new wood, and after his first use of it, used nothing else except for his mirror frames and wall brackets which, as they were to be gilded, were made of pine. This is a softer wood and better adapted to the ornate rococo carving he employed for his mirror frames and brackets. It would be interesting to know something of the work Chippendale did before the intro- duction of mahogany. He was an estab- lished cabinetmaker before that time, as was his father before him, and had un- doubtedly made furniture of walnut or

Fig. 32.
Chippendale Mirror

marquetry in the then prevailing style. Some pieces made by him in walnut or marquetry may still be ex- tant, but this is in the realm of surmise. Chippendale was a wood-carver by trade, the son of a wood-carver, and the natural result was that he developed the art of carving to its highest plane on wood so suitable to it as mahogany. This was most important, as carving had gone almost out of fashion, having given way to the vogue of inlay and marquetry. There is no authentic piece of Chippendale furniture in which inlay or mar- quetry was originally used, although some of his and other contemporaneous pieces were later "improved" by inserting inlay, but the very presence of such "im- provements" proves that they were not in the original piece. And for his carving he had the genius to per- ceive with unerring eye the best design to be used for the character of the wood. Instead of reverting to the elaborate carving of the Tudor Period, beautiful and distinctive as it was, and admirably suited to the

English oak which was used, he chose the style of Grinling Gibbons, whose wonderfully delicate carving, undercut and pierced, seemed almost detached from the background. Grinling Gibbons lived at the end of the Seventeenth Century, and although his work was largely architectural and was used for the decoration of panelling, etc., there are still preserved some beautiful examples of furniture made by him. Even more than by Grinling Gibbons he was influenced by the contemporaneous French styles, modifying them to give the work a character and individuality of his own. In the general designs he was influenced largely by the contemporaneous French fashions, and to a greater extent by the old Gothic examples and by the Chinese. Trade with China was being carried on by the hardy mariners of the times, and many pieces of furniture

Fig. 33. Chippendale Table, in the "Chinese Taste" (authentic).

were included in the cargoes. The influence of these in Chippendale's work is seen in the delicate pieces in the "Chinese Taste."

In this connection it may be pointed out that Chippendale was not a genius who suddenly originated a new and wonderful style. Art does not spring suddenly into being, and Chippendale's work was a development of previous styles as surely as the great works of the Italian painters, Raphael and Leonardo da Vinci, or of the architects of the Parthenon or the sculpture of Praxiteles, were the developments of early

Fig. 34. Cabriole Leg with ball and claw foot

works improved and glorified by master hands. The cabriole leg, with or without ball and claw feet, so often seen in chairs by Chippendale, was not originated by him, but was used in simpler forms in previous periods. It was, however, developed and beautified by him to suit his own material. In his later chairs, Chippendale did not use the cabriole leg, but developed the straight leg, sometimes molded, often solid or with beading running up and down, and made with or without cross pieces near the floor. The result was a chair of more apparent strength and solidity.

Objection is made by some furniture lovers that the furniture made by Chippendale was so elaborated and carved that it looks weak, giving one a sense of insecurity and an instinctive feeling that these beautiful chairs were made not for use, but for exhibition only. It was certainly more delicate and refined than any furniture produced prior to that time, but the fact that it has survived nearly 200 years, during many of which it was in actual use, seems the best answer to this objection.

The tables produced by this master were of various types. The shell edge or pie crust table, arranged so that the top can be turned to a vertical position was one of his favorite designs. He also made various types of square tables, the delicate, slender large or small "occasional" table with or without grating or low railing at top and with square or cabriole legs; the heavy, carved "sideboard" table, with carving reminiscent of Grinling Gibbons; tables in the "Chinese Taste"; as well as "butterfly" tables, made to close up, similar to the gate leg table, were among his best and most characteristic work.

But it was in the designing and making of chairs, undoubtedly his best work, that Chippendale is best known. He made them both with and without arms, with the legs and backs of various designs. The seats were generally stuffed. The legs included claw and ball

SOME CHIPPENDALE CHAIR BACKS

Fig. 35. Ribbon   Fig. 36. Gothic   Fig. 37. Chinese   Fig. 38. Ladder

or spade feet; the square leg, sometimes plain, sometimes molded or beaded; the carved lattice leg in the "Chinese Taste"; the fretwork Gothic leg and the leg inspired by the French rococo, but modified and lacking the extravagance, and meaningless carvings of the

[30]

French. All of these types had a charm of their own and were essentially Chippendale. The backs also showed a beautiful feeling of design. These included the Gothic, always very elaborate, sometimes resembling church windows and traceries; the Chinese, which was often geometrical; the ladder back; the wheel back, and the exquisite ribbon back, delicate as a piece of fine old lace.

In this connection mention should also be made of his settees. The most beautiful of these consisted of two conjoined chairs, with intricate backs, legs and arms, and representing both the highest development of the English imitation of the "Chinese Taste" and the elaborate ribbon back type. Often these settees had both the back and seat covered with rep of a dull black or orange color, the legs being of the cabriole type.

In the designing of mirrors Chippendale was influenced more by the French rococo style than in any of his other work, modifying the detail of these in many cases to give it a finer character. Not finding any necessity for apparent or real structural lines in mirror frames, such as are needed in chairs or tables, he made them purely fanciful and ornamental, so justifying the name of "English Rococo," applied to his work by some writers. To make them even richer, he gilded the

Fig. 39. Chippendale Settee

Fig. 40. Room from Philadelphia, Pennsylvania, showing Chippendale chair and tables, also wing sofa and interesting grandfather's clock.

Fig. 41. Mahogany Sideboard, 1790-1800. Sheraton influence. The beauty of line of this handsome piece explains the fine reproductions made of it by modern makers.

ornate carving and woodwork, in some cases decorating them with paintings.

Many beautiful bookcases and bookcase desks were also among the finest examples of his work. These were made in a variety of designs with doors or drawers in the lower section, and generally with the upper section arranged with glazed doors, the glass being divided into geometrical designs by means of small wooden moldings. The part of the desk back of the drop shelf was divided into most ingenious and attractive pigeonholes. In many examples, the upper glazed section was omitted. The tops of the glazed portion were sometimes inlaid and richly carved, and sometimes with broken pediments, either straight or curved. Fire screens, dressing tables, various types of clocks, beds and whatnots, also called dumbwaiters, were made by him in the same characteristic manner.

Chippendale's work was important not only on account of the admirable character of the individual pieces produced by him, but even more so on account of the influence his work had on the work of contemporaneous and later furniture makers, both in England and America. Authentic pieces by him are rare. Many pieces are probably by him, but in lieu of the lack of absolute proof, the museums, with commendable honesty and tact, label them "In the Style of Chippendale." Work in the character of this period is being made most successfully by modern American furniture makers with all the grace and character of the early prototypes.

The next work in this period of furniture was that of the Adam Brothers, Hepplewhite and Sheraton. The designs were to a great extent influenced by Chippendale, except in the case of the Adam Brothers, whose work was influenced more by the new Classic Revival following the discoveries in Pompeii and by the work of the Romans which the Adam Brothers studied in Italy.

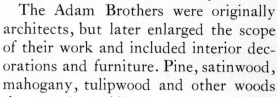

The Adam Brothers were originally architects, but later enlarged the scope of their work and included interior decorations and furniture. Pine, satinwood, mahogany, tulipwood and other woods were used by them, and combined or used together, produced rich and sumptuous effects. Nevertheless, there are also preserved pieces of pine or other simpler woods, used in a dignified manner, with formal carving in the style that might be called Classical. Often the panels were decorated by Angelica Kauffman and other celebrated artists of the day.

Fig. 42. Shield Back—
Hepplewhite

George Hepplewhite, concerning whose life very little is known, and who died in 1786, is, with the exception of Chippendale, the best known maker of English mahogany furniture as distinct from inlaid mahogany. It is very difficult to assign any particular piece of furniture to him and to say that it was made by him, but his book, which was published two years after his death, had a far-reaching influence on the other furniture manufacturers of the time. His work was more delicate and refined than that of Chippendale, and, like him, he did not resort to inlay, although he did introduce the use of thin lines of a lighter wood around the edge of panels as was done later by Sheraton. His work was characterized by lightness and delicacy of detail, even to the extreme of seeming frail. It was, however, structurally sound. Hepplewhite was the first to use the shield back chair; also the rosettes at the corners of the panels, the moldings of the panels being curved around these rosettes. The basis for his ornamentation were the wheat ear, the honeysuckle flower, or the feathers taken from the coat of arms of the Prince of Wales.

The principal pieces made by Hepplewhite were chairs, as was also the case with Chippendale, but they were generally very much lighter than his predecessors, and instead of using the cabriole leg or square leg he introduced the use of a tapered leg, very graceful and light. Hepplewhite was also very fond of using the winged easy chair with wings on either side of the back the same height as the back. This chair was generally upholstered or covered with material, the wood of the legs being the only woodwork exposed. In addition to the work which he did in mahogany, he also was influenced by the Adam Brothers, and used satinwood with painted festoons or flowers. These were undoubtedly very beautiful, but it is an unfortunate fact that the woodwork so ornamented is not improved with age, as is the case with inlaid wood. The paint decoration quickly wears off and if it is renewed it is often done by someone who has neither the artistic skill nor the sense of color of the original artist. Included in his work were also knife boxes, inlaid tea caddies and other small pieces of furniture.

Thomas Sheraton, born 1751—died 1806, was the next outstanding figure among the great furniture makers of England. He was a rare combination of artist, inventor, religious mystic and furniture maker.

Always a dreamer, and not at all practical, he was never a success financially, and his family was always in want. He published a book on the religious controversies of the time before he published his book on furniture. The character of his work was influenced somewhat by Chippendale and Hepplewhite, but even more so by the productions of the Louis XVI Period in France and by his artistic sense and his keen desire for color. He was an artist first, then a cabinetmaker. The forms were rather severe with most delicate inlay of beautifully blended colors, very little carving and then only in low relief. Very frequently his enrichments were painted on the wood, making for gracefulness and lightness. He was, next to Chippendale, undoubtedly the most remarkable man in the history of English furniture.

It is an unfortunate fact that only one piece of furniture, a glass-fronted bookcase, can be definitely attributed to him, but the style and designs illustrated and described in his books were made in large numbers by the other manufacturers of the day. He was very fond of the use of satinwood, kingwood and tulipwood, and is thought to have been the first to use "harewood," which is a sycamore wood cut to show a beautiful grain and dyed a delicate pale shade of brown. The beauty of this wood when dyed, possibly also suggested to him the staining of portions of light wood in a beautiful green color. He was the first to use the screen table, a table which can be also used as a screen, making it beautiful and practical.

Mention should also be made of the names of Shearer, Ince and Mayhew, Mainwaring, and Copeland. While not so celebrated nor as well known as Chippendale,

Hepplewhite, Sheraton and the Adam Brothers, books or catalogues they produced had considerable influence on the prevailing styles, and if their names had not been overshadowed by those of the greater masters, they would have received a more prominent place in the history of English furniture.

The Eighteenth Century undoubtedly produced the greatest work in the designing and execution of furniture, not only in England but also in France, where the style of Louis XVI, more restrained than the preceding style of Louis XIV and XV, and influenced to a great extent by the Classic Revival, produced examples worthy of a place in the finest museums. This was due to a great extent to the fact that the principal manufacturers published books of designs which were used by the other manufacturers of the times, and thus beautiful ideas were multiplied. Aside from the making of furniture this is important, as we are able

Fig. 43. Chippendale Chair   Fig. 44. Hepplewhite Chair   Fig. 45. Adam Brothers Chair   Fig. 46. Sheraton Chair

to give credit where credit is due. About this time in America the same was true of architecture, and our beautiful Colonial homes, built in the Colonial style, were the direct result of books published by masters, and serving as examples for the carpenters and workmen.

Fig. 47. Early American Oak Chest, 1650-1675. Note the heavy
character of this piece of furniture and the all-over carving.

Fig. 48. Mahogany Chest of Drawers, 1750-1775. American ex-
ample of the block-front type.

III

American Furniture

AFTER all, the most important furniture, as far as we Americans are concerned, is the American of Colonial style, interesting not only because it is our own successful development and adaptation of preceding styles, but also because it is obtainable either in the original pieces or in the beautiful and well made reproductions of which so many of our leading furniture manufacturers make a specialty, many examples of which are illustrated in the portfolio in the back of this book.

While a great portion of Colonial furniture may justly be called "In the Style of Chippendale," Hepplewhite, or other English furniture makers, it is, nevertheless, true that the American productions, although inspired by the books of these English masters, were executed in a manner different from the English types and with a characteristic artistic feeling of their own. This was especially true of the Colonial reproductions in the Chippendale style. Our sturdy ancestors used only his more vigorous and dignified types and did not make furniture in the frail and elaborate "Chinese Taste." In the American "Style of Sheraton" furniture, while it is evident that his book was the source of inspiration, the change was in the direction of greater vigor and solidity. An expert can readily distinguish between a piece made in America and one made in England. Later, when the Revolutionary War had left so much bitter feeling between the former colonies and their mother country, the American designers turned to the French Empire style for examples. This is especially true of the work of Duncan Phyfe, which will be discussed later.

The finest Colonial furniture was undoubtedly made

Fig. 49   Fig. 50

Fig. 49. Walnut Highboy, 1700-1710. Later developed into the more elaborate highboy as shown in other illustrations.

Fig. 50. Mahogany Desk with reversed serpentine foot and cabinet top. American, 1765-1780.

in Philadelphia, where from about the year 1725 to the end of the Revolutionary War there were master cabinetmakers, among them being Randolph, Gillingham and Savery. There was also much excellent furniture being made in Alexandria, Virginia, in Baltimore, in Boston, in Annapolis, and Newport, Rhode Island, where John Goddard made a specialty of desks and chests of drawers.

In this connection it may be well to speak on the subject of antique furniture, both foreign and American. While it is true that there are many real old pieces and that many families are the proud possessors of genuine heirlooms inherited from their forefathers, it is an indisputable fact that the number of these authentic pieces is limited.

It is self-evident that not enough furniture was made in the olden times to satisfy the modern craving for antiques, with the result that in order to satisfy this desire, spurious antiques are sold as the genuine article. This is perhaps easier to accomplish because the seeker of old furniture, unless he be an expert, cannot differentiate between the real and the imitation. Furthermore, after he has bought the imitation he has the very human characteristic of "standing up for his own" and resenting any suggestion that the piece may be a fraud. The writer recalls that about fifteen years ago he spent some years in rural Pennsylvania, and being interested in the subject of old furniture, made inquiry in the neighborhood, in an endeavor to find some. The neighborhood seemed promising as there were quite a few houses there from one hundred to two hundred years old. He was informed that the entire countryside had been "swept dry" of these articles years before. About ten years later he revisited the same neighborhood and was amazed to find "antique furniture" with pieces beautifully made and of a character to deceive any one except an expert. In Venice some years ago, while exploring a bystreet, he found a furniture factory where they were making the most beautiful reproductions of Italian furniture imaginable, so well made that even an expert would be deceived. One of the workmen, who had been in America, in-

Fig. 51. Banister Back Arm Chair, 1700-1725. Maple and ash with oak arms. This chair has the sawed balusters, spade feet and rush seat.

formed him with a grin that this furniture was being made for the American market, to be sold as "Italian antique furniture." The business, he said, was very profitable. It is better to pay a fair price for an honest well-made reproduction with good lines and of good design than to pay a fancy price for the same article sold under the name of "antiques." Legitimate and honest reproductions are being made in large number by leading furniture manufacturers and sold as reproductions. This

[42]

places these beautiful examples within the reach of all.

The fact that furniture is being made in this country as good as, and not distinguishable from, that made in the Eighteenth Century, speaks well for our modern manufacturers. This gives hope that, with proper encouragement from discriminating patrons, distinctly American furniture may be produced that will not be merely a reproduction of the old, but of a character original and alive. By this is meant not freakish or *art nouveau* but an adaptation of earlier American styles, with good lines and ornament and characteristic of our modern life.

The early furniture made in America was similar to the furniture of the William and Mary style in England, influenced to a great extent by the Dutch examples. It was generally of straight lines and the different members fitted into each other, at right angles. The early chests, which have a massive character, had heavy corner posts, so that the body of the chest was four or five inches above the ground. The entire surface was covered with flat, crude carving. In some cases corners were chamfered. These were generally of oak. Later these chests were developed into chests of drawers on turned legs, and sometimes turned stretchers, and still later they developed into the high chest of drawers of walnut with the inverted baluster legs, and later into our well known highboy.

The characteristic piece of American furniture is the corner cupboard, sometimes painted, and sometimes, although not often, of mahogany. The upper part of these was fitted with glazed doors divided into panels of various designs with wooden muntins, the lower part being arranged as cupboards with wooden doors. They

[43]

Fig. 52. Virginia Walnut Lowboy, by William Savery, 1760-1775.

Fig. 53. Room from "Marmion," Prince George County, Virginia. Furniture is American Colonial showing Chippendale influence. It is interesting to see how the cabriole leg and ball and claw foot tend to harmonize the different pieces of furniture. The mirror is Chippendale and the style of the furniture is of the most elaborate of this period made in America.

were among the most interesting pieces of furniture made in this country.

The earliest tables consisted of large boards on trestles. These were generally of pine or oak, and were left without any paint or finish. Later the chair table, of which the top hinged back to form a chair, the lower drawer forming the seat, and the posts which extended from the top of the seat forming the arms. The butterfly table and the well-known hundred-legged table, with twisted legs and with part of the top made to fall down and form a pier table, came next. Later the small walnut tables with a simple cab-riole leg, following plainly the Dutch influence, the pie crust table and the mahogany tables "in the style of Chippendale, Hepplewhite or Sheraton." These adapta-tions of English designs, while they follow to a great extent the designs published in the books of the English furniture manufacturers, are characteristically true Amer-ican, as their prototypes are characteristically English.

The earliest chairs made in this country were the chairs similar to the Tudor chairs previously described, with the triangular seat with turned members. About the same period was the wainscot chair, which later developed into a chair with turned legs and stretchers, the seats and back covered with material. Later came the Dutch influence chairs, with cane inserts in seat and back; and the banister back chair, the lower part of which was similar to the Dutch chairs of the time, the back being formed of turned banisters cut in half with the smooth side turned to support the back. These were characteristically American, the cut baluster showing perhaps too much a spirit of economy.

Fig. 54. American Mirrors, 1790-1800. Showing the use of the eagle and the American flag.

One class of chairs which deserves particular mention is the Windsor chair, which was first made in this country at the end of the Eighteenth Century. The origin of this design is not known, but there is a legend that one of the King Georges first found this chair in a peasant's house, near Windsor, England, and that it immediately became popular there. It was first made in Philadelphia about 1763, being widely advertised at that time by a cabinetmaker, who called himself a Windsor chair manufacturer. The earliest forms consisted of the arms secured around the back with an extension top with either end fastened into the arms and supported by means of spindles, the legs being turned. Later the arms and back were formed of bent wood supported by spindles, this becoming the best known form. Subsequently to this, the chair was made with rectangular lines following in general shape the

[46]

shape of the chairs of the Sheraton school. Windsor chairs, which were generally painted, were the everyday chair of these times, and often colored to suit the individual taste of the owner. The English Windsor chair differed from the American Colonial in that they sometimes had a splat back, which was never used by the American cabinetmakers. Also, the turning of the legs and rungs was simpler and less elaborate in the American chair. In fact, some of the English Windsor chairs have cabriole legs with claw feet.

Fig. 55. Windsor Arm Chairs, showing the round high extension back, and a Sheraton influence extension back. 1750-1775.

The chairs made in this country in the style of Chippendale, Sheraton and Hepplewhite were Colonial in character and are, with the possible exception of the desks and highboys, the most successful examples of Colonial furniture.

[47]

Fig. 56. Mahogany Highboy, 1760-1775, by William Savery of Philadelphia. One of the best examples of this maker, who did much to give Philadelphia the reputation of making the finest furniture in Colonial America.

The sideboards also were developments of the early cupboards and the most beautiful examples of these, particularly in the Sheraton and Hepplewhite style, were of such exquisite design that the originators of these styles would undoubtedly have been glad to call them their own make. Particularly is this true of the delicate Sheraton style sideboards, with their fine lines of inlay, beautifully selected mahogany veneering and brass handles.

The mirrors made in this country were in many cases similar to the ornate Chippendale and Adam mirrors but simpler and with less feeling of the rococo, but the plain mirror with the wide mahogany frame with some gilt ornament or eagle on the top and gilt ornament on the side, was characteristically American, and most successful.

The clocks included the small mantel clocks of mahogany as well as reproductions of the tall "grandfather's clock," as beautiful as any made in England at this time. In this connection mention should be made of the Willard or banjo clock and similar types. These were made by the various members of the Willard family at the end of the Eighteenth Century and consisted of the small mantel clock and particularly of the banjo-shaped clocks, often in mahogany, enriched with brass moldings or with painting. The work of the Willards is charming and original, especially the banjo clocks, and marks an epoch in the designing of these pieces. Original clocks by these masters are highly prized by collectors who are fortunate enough to obtain them.

Knife and spoon boxes, sometimes vase-shaped, wine

coolers, candlesticks and other small pieces of furniture were also made of a character to correspond with the furniture on which they were to rest.

There seems to be some difference of opinion among lovers of the antique as to the first use of the rocking chair. Many old examples of rockers consisted of old side or arm chairs with the bottoms of the legs cut off and rockers applied at some later date. There are, however, a few authentic examples of old chairs in which the rockers were undoubtedly part of the original design. Among these are some very beautiful Windsor chairs.

Perhaps the most successful pieces of furniture made in this country were the desks, both high and low. These are preserved to us in a great variety. There is the high desk or secretary with drawers and writing cabinet underneath and glazed or wooden doors in the upper portion, sometimes with straight broken pediment, sometimes with the curved broken pediment, sometimes with the curved broken pediment for the upper portion, also with formal brass statuary or urns in connection with the pediment. The low desks were similar to the high ones, often made of the "block front" type.

Mahogany seems to have been used in this country, although not to a large extent, even before it was used in England. There are some authentic Colonial pieces antedating by about twenty years the first piece that Chippendale made. This was not unnatural, as the West Indies, one source of mahogany, are closer to America than to England. It is most fortunate that the Santo Domingo mahogany tree, which is of very slow growth and which for a time threatened to become extinct, is now being cultivated and the wood is obtainable in as beautiful a grain as the antique, and is being used in the manufacturing of the better class furniture.

It is fortunate that walnut is also plentiful and can be obtained in wood as beautifully grained and of as good color as any used in the olden time. This is important, as certain types of furniture and reproductions require the soft subdued color of this beautiful wood, which vies with mahogany in its durability and its improvement with age.

The Colonial cabinetmakers also used birch, pearwood and maple, entire sets of bedroom furniture in this latter wood being most eagerly sought by collectors, who appreciate and prize the beautiful and mellow tone, which is the result of age.

After the Revolutionary War and early in the Nineteenth Century the popular American style was in mahogany, of a heavy character known as American Empire. This is characterized by the beautifully grained crotch veneer, by heavy scroll supports, and often by brass or gilded enrichments.

American furniture up to the early part of the Nineteenth Century is named for its period or design and it was not until about 1800 that the name of any one man was applied to a style. At that time Duncan Phyfe, a Scotchman, who had a furniture shop in Partition Street, New York City, and later in Fulton Street, made furniture which was original and characteristic enough so that the name of "Duncan Phyfe Design" may correctly be applied to it. While he was influenced to a great extent by the Sheraton style in his early work, he later became influenced more by the Empire style. His work is characterized by beautiful carving and reeding and, while he worked principally with mahogany, in some of his pieces he obtained color effects by the combination of beautiful woods used together with the mahogany. Phyfe was the fashionable cabinetmaker of his time and many rich New Yorkers were among his patrons. He introduced in the back of chairs and sofas a lyre of which the strings were brass and also used this same motif in the supports of his tables. He made a card table with four legs, one of which, by an interesting mechanism, was folded in when half of the circular top was folded over the other half, and it became a pier table. He had many imitators in his time.

One of the characteristics of American furniture of the early Nineteenth Century was the use of the eagle, sometimes in the backs of chairs, on mirrors, often as the supports of tables and in the pediments of bookcases. This was a natural result of the Revolutionary War and of the patriotic spirit then so prevalent in this country. When used in the backs of chairs or on mirrors the eagle was frequently gilded but the most impressive examples are the larger than life-size ones, full of action and spirit, which were used as the supports of pier tables or of large tables.

IV

Construction of Furniture

THE method of constructing furniture has not
changed materially since the introduction of
veneering and gluing, if we except the natural
saving of time and labor due to the use of machinery.
In the early periods, that is, up to about the middle of
the Seventeenth Century, the different parts were put
together by means of mortise and tenon; that is, one
member was provided with a projecting piece or tenon
while the other member to which it was to be fitted,
had a corresponding hole in it of the same size. After
the tenon was fitted into the mortise, wooden pins,
generally of oak, were used to hold the two pieces together. This method of making furniture is characteristic of furniture of these early periods, and furniture
put together in the modern way and labeled as being
made before this time is probably not what it claims
to be. When glue was used together with veneers the
wooden pins were dispensed with and the different members were held together by means of glue, sometimes
with mortise and tenon and sometimes merely abutting.

In this connection it may be well to discuss furniture
made "in the old way" as compared to the furniture
made "by modern methods." If by modern methods is
meant using wood that is not properly seasoned and

[53]

Fig. 57. Duncan Phyfe Sofa, Chairs and Table, showing use of the lyre with brass strings so characteristic of this maker.

Fig. 58   Fig. 59

Figs. 58 and 59 Mahogany Arm and Side Chairs, 1785-1795. Hepplewhite influence; preserving all the grace of the English prototype but more sturdy in character.

not properly fastened together there is no comparison possible. If, however, the wood is thoroughly seasoned and dried and the different parts put together firmly and in workmanlike manner, there is no reason why furniture made in the modern way should not stand as well as the antique hand-made furniture. The fact that the lathes in modern days are turned by machinery instead of by foot-power, and that different parts are sawed out with machinery, instead of being slowly and laboriously worked out by hand, makes no difference in the ultimate piece of wood, assuming always that it is thoroughly seasoned and dried. It is true that the furniture made entirely by hand had a certain unevenness in the moldings and variations in the different pieces of carving when they were repeated. But these variations, if they are wanted to please the eye, can easily be made after the wood leaves the machine. Furniture made of wood in the proper condition, mortised and tenoned, glued and finished with du Pont Duco to protect it from the weather, will last indefinitely, whether the different parts have been fashioned into the required shape by hand or machine. In fact, modern machinery, hydraulic presses for veneering, waterproof glue and stronger joints, make modern furniture structurally sounder than the antique. It must also be borne in mind that at the present time we have the advantage of a larger selection of woods.

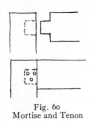
Fig. 60
Mortise and Tenon

V

Furniture Finishes

THE manner of finishing furniture has varied with and been one of the characteristics of different periods of furniture. For instance, early English furniture was finished "natural," that is, a transparent finish which in time mellowed and was a forerunner of the modern "fumed oak" finish. Gilt furniture is generally associated with the Louis XIV and Louis XV styles. Italian Renaissance furniture was sometimes finished "natural," sometimes painted, even to the extent of having pictures painted in the panels, and often gilded.

While it is almost impossible to obtain the actual facts about the initial development of finishing the very early pieces in England, the interesting conjecture has been made that on the first pieces of furniture no pretense was made of protecting the wood in any way. But in the days when knights and high-born damsels used their fingers for forks and daggers for knives, grease from boars' heads and vension dripped on the raw wood, and some progressive baron noticed that in this way his table was not only beautified but also protected. Therefore when a new table was delivered, the surface came well rubbed with grease.

In France before the time of Louis XIV the finish

known in modern times as "French polish" was developed. This was no more than the saturation of the wood with coat after coat of oil. Almost simultaneously other artificers discovered that the continued applications of wax made a beautiful surface on furniture.

Varnish and paint were known in the Middle Ages; in fact, the major part of these commodities were made in monasteries which controlled the formulæ.

Fig. 61. Mahogany Tilt Table, 1760-1775. Chippendale influence.

The different methods of finishing which were in vogue for centuries are as follows:

Varnish, a composition of linseed oil and gums which dries by oxidization. It is sometimes applied directly to the wood, sometimes with a coat of shellac under it. As the finish oxidizes it deteriorates. This is manifested either by the checking or cracking of the finish, the dulling of its lustre, and a tendency to flake off with age.

Fig. 62. Parlor from Home in Haverhill, Mass. Note the grandfather's clock and shield back Hepplewhite chair.

Because of its composition it is also easily scratched. It becomes soft under heat so that it "prints" or takes the impression of objects placed upon it. "Tacky" varnish will also stick to clothes in warm weather. Water, either hot or cold, will affect varnish, quickly destroying the original beauty of the finish.

Painted finish, consisting of white lead and linseed oil mixed in the proper proportions with color added to give the desired tone, and requiring for good work four or five coats. Paint of which the base was white lead and linseed oil and in which the coloring matter was yellow ochre, indigo, lampblack and similar materials was known and used by the ancient Greeks and Romans, and in later times until the time of the Italian Renaissance when the furniture was finished "natural," i.e., to show the grain of the wood, with the exception of some pieces which were painted and decorated. Painted or gilded furniture was later made in France in the times of Louis XIV, Louis XV and Louis XVI. Some of the Adams Brothers furniture, as well as the American Windsor chairs and other early American furniture was painted, but with these exceptions a transparent finish was usually used.

Lacquer finish, so-called, is available in two forms. It may consist of shellac dissolved in alcohol with coloring matter added. It was largely used by the Chinese and those who copied their style of furniture. The old "lacquer" work of the Chinese and Japanese was done with the juice of a tree similar to our sumac, mixed with other ingredients to obtain the desired color, and produced by means of successive coats a highly polished lustrous surface. More modern lacquer finishes are made from nitrocellulose.

Wax finish is another finishing method consisting of beeswax applied in several coats and rubbed. This method of finishing, applied year after year, was the one used by the famous furniture makers of the Eighteenth Century to obtain the beautiful finish on mahogany, the only disadvantage being that it requires years of patient care and effort to obtain its full beauty.

The most modern method of finishing, however, represents a radical change, not only in the materials used but also in the durability secured. Chemists have evolved a finish from cotton* which is beautiful but also lasts very much longer than any other material hitherto available. This finish has been in use on automobiles for several years under the most trying exposure to every possible weather condition.

[*Editor's Note:* On furniture, the new finish is a blessing to the housewife. It means that the finish will not lose its lustre, growing duller with years. To keep it looking new, it is only necessary to use a damp cloth instead of messy, smelly, sticky polishes. In extreme cases, the finish may be most satisfactorily washed with soap and water. The new material is impervious to either hot or cold liquids. Spilled ice water or hot coffee will not ruin the finish on a beautiful piece of furniture, as was the case with other finishing materials. This du Pont *Duco* finish is also hard to scratch or mar and cannot get soft or sticky under heat. There is no danger

---

*Duco is made only by the du Pont Company, Parlin, N. J. It is a pyroxylin mixture with cotton as a base. This cotton is chemically treated by nitration so as to become soluble in certain solvents. Because of its basic material, it is sometimes referred to as "liquid cotton."

of "tackiness" or "printing." This material is available either clear or colored and is now being used by a large number of American manufacturers. In all probability, your own furniture dealer can give you any additional information you may require about this unusual finish. So radical is this change in the finishing of furniture that furniture experts are beginning to call the present era of furniture the "*Duco* Period." They point out that for the first time the finish is now almost as durable as the wood itself—in fact, the finish becomes an integral part of a piece of furniture and not merely a surface coating which protects the wood only a comparatively short time. Those interested in furniture claim that, as characteristic designs created the earlier periods, so this radical change in furniture is the hallmark by which the present period in furniture will be known in the future.]